Canyons, Gullies, and Slots (E)—Arizona is perhaps best known for its canyons, which form by the action of running water, typically rivers and streams. Many people are surprised to learn this since Arizona has few rivers. However, it is not the day-to-day trickle of water that creates canyons. Rather it is the huge, infrequent floods that move boulders and tear away at the bedrock to deepen canyons. And as canyons become deeper, their walls become oversteepened and the process of upslope retreat acts to widen canyons. Gullies (from Latin ***gula***, meaning "throat") are small canyons. Slot canyons are very narrow defiles that in many instances form when an earlier canyon becomes blocked with sediment causing water to find a new route. The word canyon is from the Spanish ***cañon***, meaning a large hollow or tube.

The best example of a canyon in Arizona is the Grand Canyon (**CP**)—*one mile deep, ten miles wide and 277 miles long! It is one of the Seven Natural Wonders of the World. But Arizona is also home to Canyon de Chelly* (**CP**), *Black Canyon (where Hoover Dam is located)* (**BR**), *Antelope Canyon* (**CP**), *Oak Creek Canyon* (**CP**) *and the Salt River Canyon* (**TZ**).

An Introduction to Arizona Landforms

The state of Arizona is blessed with a multitude of interesting and intriguing landforms. From the red rock buttes of Monument Valley to the "sky island" mountain ranges in the southern deserts, Arizona's landscape continues to draw the praise of advertisers, scientists, travelers and poets. The arid climate leaves landforms here generally unencumbered by trees or other vegetation, making them easily observable and a welcome amenity in any outdoor adventure. Landforms by definition are the naturally produced surface features of the earth's crust. They provide the interested observer with endless opportunities to learn something about how the Arizona landscape came to be.

The creation of these landforms tells a fascinating story. It involves a mind-boggling parade of ancient environments that left behind a thick stack of stratified sediment. This colorful sediment originated in shallow tropical seas, sandy desert dunes, or ancient rivers that in some instances originated in the Appalachia hundreds of millions of years ago. This is the ***depositional*** phase of Arizona's geologic story and it created the "canvas" upon which the landforms were "painted." Arizona's rocks were eventually uplifted a few vertical miles, initiating the ***erosional*** phase of the state's geologic story. Many landforms today result from the interaction of these erosional processes acting on preexisting rocks. The last few million years have produced an "icing" on the cake—eruptions of lava related to a ***volcanic*** phase in the development of landforms. The cake itself includes many canyons, buttes, spires and mesas so common in this state.

Arizona's Geologic Provinces

Arizona is divided into three distinct geologic regions or provinces. In the northern part of the state is the colorful Colorado Plateau, where the elevation is typically more than one mile above sea level and the rocks are composed mostly of stratified sediments. In the southern portion of the state is the Basin and Range, a land of many low lying valleys broken by isolated mountain ranges. The rocks here are quite variable being made of igneous, metamorphic or sedimentary types. These two provinces compose the bulk of Arizona's landscape and were separated from each other only within the last 15 to 20 million years. In the process of their parting, a third province called the Transition Zone was created. As the name implies, this narrow strip is transitional in nature, with rocks like those of the Colorado Plateau being deformed in a manner like the Basin and Range.

Certain landforms may be more commonly found in a particular province but there is overlap, and a few, like mesas or canyons, are common in each province. Canyons, mesas, buttes and spires are the more dominant landforms in the Colorado Plateau. Mountains, valleys, playas and alluvial fans dominate the Basin and Range. The Transition Zone has volcanic mesas, mountains and canyons. Landforms created by erosion will have (**E**) next to them, those formed by deposition (**D**) and volcanic (**V**). Some landforms may be the result of two processes. Specific landforms mentioned in this book will have the abbreviation (**CP**), (**BR**), and (**TZ**) to denote which province that feature belongs to. All landforms may seem "everlasting" to us but they are forever changing and evolving.

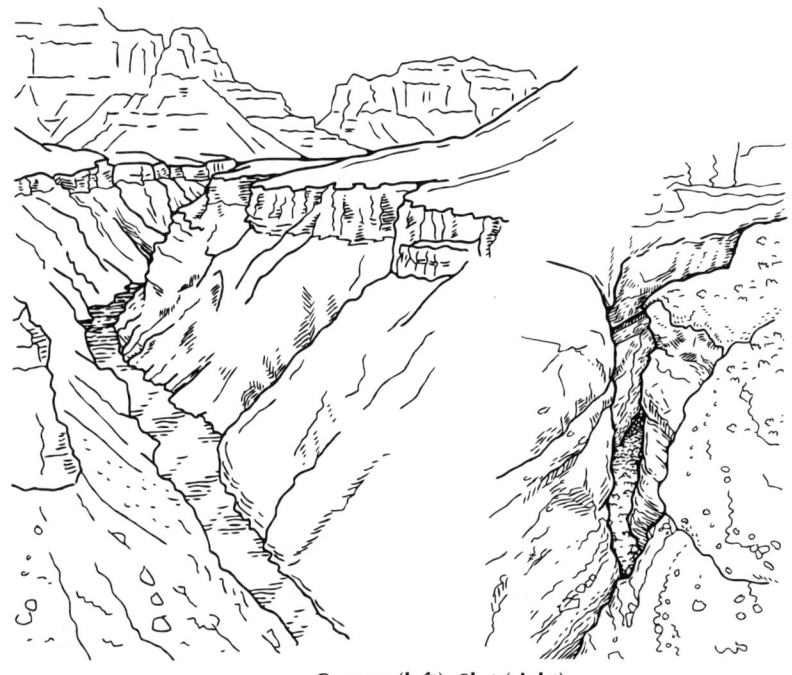

Canyon (left), Slot (right)

Mesas, Buttes and Spires (E) and (D)—Observers will find some Arizona landforms have exceedingly flat tops. These are the many mesas (Spanish for "table") and buttes that dot the landscape. To create these, alternating layers of hard rock such as sandstone and soft rock such as shale are needed. These were widely deposited on featureless surfaces where gravity created horizontal layers. Erosion removes the overlying shale exposing a hard layer of sandstone—a mesa is thus created. Erosion continually attacks the edges of mesas and as rocks progressively fall off they become narrower through time. Once the height of a mesa equals its width, it is called a butte. As erosion attacks the edges of a butte, it becomes more tall than it is wide and a spire (or monument, tower or pinnacle) is created. Thus, mesas become buttes and buttes become spires! (Note: Not every 19th century prospector who named a landform knew the rules and sometimes names for mesas or buttes are interchanged).

*Black Mesa (**CP**) may be the largest in Arizona at over 70 miles but mesas come in all sizes. The Mittens (**CP**) in Monument Valley are perhaps the most photographed buttes in the state. Spider Rock (**CP**) in Canyon de Chelly is an example of a spire. As mesas evolve into buttes and spires, they are destroyed but erosion may continue to attack other layers below, starting the process all over again.*

Spire (upper left), Butte (right), Mesa (bottom)

Cliff or Escarpment (**E**)—Some of the most prominent landforms in Arizona are cliffs or escarpments. These are steep, vertical outcroppings of rock that can sometimes stretch for great distances (100 miles or more) across the landscape. They form barriers to travel and in historic times routes or roads often followed these linear features. Their outcrop pattern reveals an association with faults or folds (see pages 10 and 11)—as one part of the earth's crust is uplifted along a fault or fold, a line of cliffs may rise parallel to the trace of it. Erosion sometimes causes a whole line of cliffs to retreat away from a fault, creating a fault line scarp.

*Some spectacular examples of escarpments or cliffs in Arizona are the Mogollon Rim (**CP**), the Echo and Vermilion cliffs (**CP**), the Comb Ridge on the east side of Monument Valley (**CP**), and the Apache Leap near Superior and the Superstition Mountain front (**TZ**), facing the Salt River Valley or Phoenix basin.*

Faults and Folds—Arizona's landscape experienced dramatic changes beginning 70 million years ago when the entire state was uplifted through squeezing of the earth's crust. Many faults (fractures) and folds (bending) were emplaced in the rocks at this time. Within the Colorado Plateau, the rock layers were bent or folded as the region was gently deformed. These folds occurred at depth but more recent erosion has brought these steeply tilted folds to the surface where they are called monoclines. Beginning between 15 and 20 million years ago, the Basin and Range was created when older, high-standing mountains were severely faulted. The many valleys and mountains in this area formed as the result of faults that lowered the valleys and raised blocks of mountains.

*The East Kaibab monocline on the eastern side of the Grand Canyon (**CP**) is an example of rocks folded at depth and exposed by erosion. The Whetstone, Chiricahua, Huachuca and Tucson mountains (**BR**) are examples of faulted blocks that were raised into ranges along fault lines—adjacent blocks are downfaulted into basins and buried by sediment.*

Fold (left), Fault (right)

Arches and Natural Bridges (**E**)—Openings in solid rock hold a fascination for all in the landscape and are known variably as arches, bridges or windows. They form in myriad ways. Bridges technically cross streams and although not too many features meet this requirement, the ones that do are magnificent. An arch does not have an association with a stream and is merely an opening into a rock. If an arch is located high in a rock wall such that the sky is seen behind it, then it might be termed a window. Arches and windows typically form in a porous rock like sandstone, where it overlies a nonporous rock like shale. Before being exposed, groundwater pools on top of the nonporous rock, weakening the cement in the porous rock. Upon exposure, an arch or window opens in the porous rock.

*Arizona is home to a spectacular natural bridge called Tonto Natural Bridge (**TZ**). Here the calcium-rich waters of Pine Creek left a hard layer of travertine (limestone deposited by spring water) on its former bed. Flood water began to eat away at the base of the travertine and eventually washed it out to create the bridge. Arches of many kinds can be found in Monument Valley, Grand Canyon and around Lake Powell (**CP**).*

Hogbacks (E)—These landforms are among the most interesting when encountered by travelers to Arizona. They have an association with the folds and monoclines of the Colorado Plateau and get their name from their tendency to form a row of undulating ridges like those found on the backs of some hogs. As once flat-lying sediment is tilted to 45 degrees or more along a fold, the strata initially form an escarpment. Through time, streams that flow off the top of the fold cut canyons that are perpendicular to the line of the fold. The canyons thus etch depressions into the line of the escarpment leaving a series of pointed ridges on the land. When viewed across the landscape they appear like a hogback.

*Hogbacks are found on the Colorado Plateau in Arizona and the most famous may be Comb Ridge (**CP**) which confines the southeastern side of Monument Valley. Other notable hogbacks can be found on portions of the Navajo Indian Reservation, including the one near the tribal capital at Window Rock, where coincidentally an arch is carved into the hogback.*

Playas or Bolsons (D)—Arizona has not always been a desert paradise. During the Ice Age, generally considered as the last two million years of earth history and ending (temporarily) only 10,000 years ago, wetter conditions prevailed across the whole state. The increased run-off that was associated with these wetter conditions was channeled in certain locations into basins without an outlet (also called bolsons). These basins today are called playas (Spanish for "beach" or "dry basin"). Sediment accumulated on the basin floor during the Ice Age and when these bolsons dried out, the sediment was exposed to the wind, creating the conditions that gave the name playa to these areas.

Playas are typically seen in the Basin and Range Province. Willcox Playa (**BR**) *southeast of Tucson is the largest playa in Arizona. Interstate 10 goes right through it west of Willcox. Red Lake, north of Kingman* (**BR**), *is another interesting playa that is underlain by thousands of feet of salt, documenting repeated evaporation of lake water through millions of years.*

Alluvial Fans and Bajadas (D)—Intense summer thunderstorms in the Basin and Range wash loads of rocky debris down mountain canyons. When this debris flows out onto the desert floor, the water trickles into the ground and drops its load of gravel and sand at the mountain front. When this area fills with rocks the stream bed is diverted to adjacent areas. Through time this process resembles a water hose as it snakes back and forth on the ground when left running free. Eventually, huge aprons of gravel and sand grace the desert floor at the foot of the mountains—an alluvial fan. Where numerous alluvial fans coalesce, they are called bajadas. Some of these lie atop tens of thousands of feet of sand and gravel. The Phoenix Basin or Salt River Valley is underlain by up to 25,000 feet of sand and gravel, testament to the filling power of alluvial fans.

Alluvial fans are best seen where steep mountain fronts meet the driest sections of the open desert. They are common in the Cabeza Prieta Wildlife Refuge and Organ Pipe Cactus National Monument (BR). Steep alluvial fans are also found along the Colorado River near Kingman (BR).

Round Granite Boulders and Spheroidal Weathering (E)—One of the more curious landforms in all of Arizona are areas of round, granite boulders that form in a process known as spheroidal weathering. Many may wonder who "piled" these boulders on the landscape, when actually they formed right where they are found. It starts when blobs of liquid magma cool slowly in the ground to form crystalline granite rock. As the granite is uplifted, it begins to fracture in myriad directions. Groundwater travels preferentially along these fracture lines and begins to disintegrate the granite here. Eventually a square or rectangular shape begins to form in the granite. Continued uplift and buffeting by the wind rounds off the edges of the squares and the landscape becomes littered with boulders.

*The Granite Dells near Prescott (**TZ**) is a great place to witness the splendors of spheroidal weathering, where boulders are created from within otherwise solid granite. Texas Canyon (**BR**) on Interstate 10 southeast of Tucson is another fascinating place to see these.*

Volcanoes and Volcanic Necks (**V**) **and** (**E**)—Arizona has all four types of volcanic cones known on planet earth. The largest are stratovolcanoes and form from many violent eruptions. Cinder cones are the smallest and form when gas-rich lava is "fountained" into the air, causing lava droplets to cool and pile around the eruptive vent. Dome volcanoes are those in which very viscous lava resists flow away from a vent and piles high around it. Shield volcanoes conversely erupt very fluid lava which flows far away from the vent, creating broad lava flows that resemble a warrior's shield laying on its side. Features known as volcanic necks form when the vent of a volcano is exposed by erosion. Most volcanic features in Arizona have formed within the last 20 to 30 million years.

*The San Francisco Peaks near Flagstaff (**CP**) represent the best example of an existing stratovolcano in the state. Sunset Crater (**CP**) is the youngest cinder cone while nearby Mt. Elden north of Flagstaff (**CP**) is the largest dome volcano. House Mountain near Sedona (**TZ**) and Glasford Hill near Prescott (**TZ**) are examples of shield volcanoes. There are numerous volcanic necks found near Kayenta such as Agathla and Church Rock (**CP**).*

Volcanic Neck (upper), Volcano (lower)

Lava and Ash Flows and Inverted Topography (V) and (E)—Surprisingly, not every volcanic eruption creates volcanoes. Lava oftentimes is so fluid that it readily flows away from the vent. In these instances, eruptions produce long-ranging lava flows, typically formed of a dense, hard rock call basalt. Basalt resists erosion, forming many black volcanic mesas in the state. Lavas that are more viscous tend to erupt violently, shattering the lava into tiny particles called ash. Oftentimes these ash flows fall to the ground while still glowing hot, producing ash layers that "weld" into a dense rock called tuff. If these lava or ash flows are emplaced in ancient valleys, the surrounding wall rocks may subsequently erode, leaving the flows as high-standing mesas known as inverted topography.

Lava flows are found in all geologic provinces in the state but some of the more recognized flows are those in Oak Creek Canyon (CP), all along Interstate 17 between the Mogollon Rim and Phoenix (TZ), and near San Carlos on the Apache Reservation (BR). Ash flows are numerous as well, and include Superstition Mountain and the Apache Leap (TZ).

Old valley with Lava Flow in bottom
Old wall
Old wall

Lava Flow on mesa top after erosion

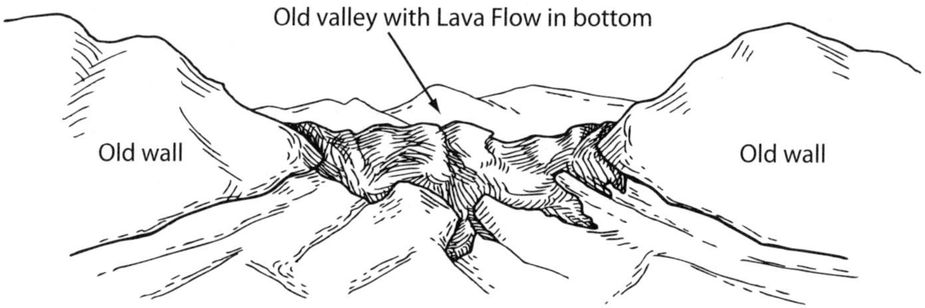

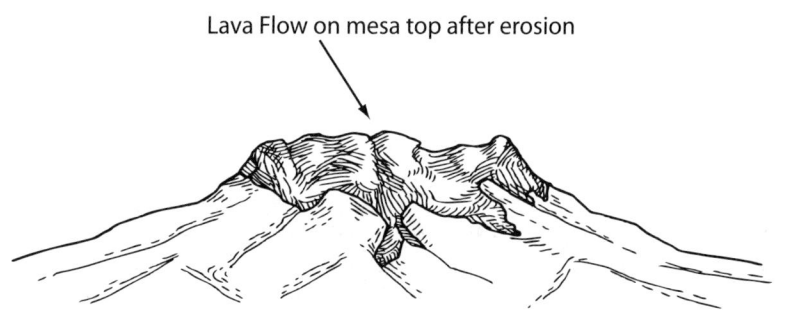

Impact Craters (E)—At least one location in Arizona is an example of a crater formed when a meteor impacted with earth's surface. These kinds of features are relatively rare on the planet (only about 172 verified) since tectonic activity and atmospheric weathering tend to obscure them through time. These features are typically circular in outline, often have upturned ridges from the impact "peeling back" the strata, and may have bits of meteoric debris lying nearby on the surface around the crater. Meteor craters are sometimes difficult to distinguish between craters that are volcanic in origin or from salt domes (that also puncture the earth's surface from below). Most impact craters however, have shocked quartz within them which can be seen in a microscope and are microscopically shattered quartz grains from the high velocity of the impactor.

West of Winslow, Meteor Crater (**CP**) *is the only known example of an impact crater in Arizona. It is about 600 feet deep and is almost one mile in diameter. The impactor fell to the earth approximately 50,000 years ago, and is estimated to have been about 100 feet in diameter.*

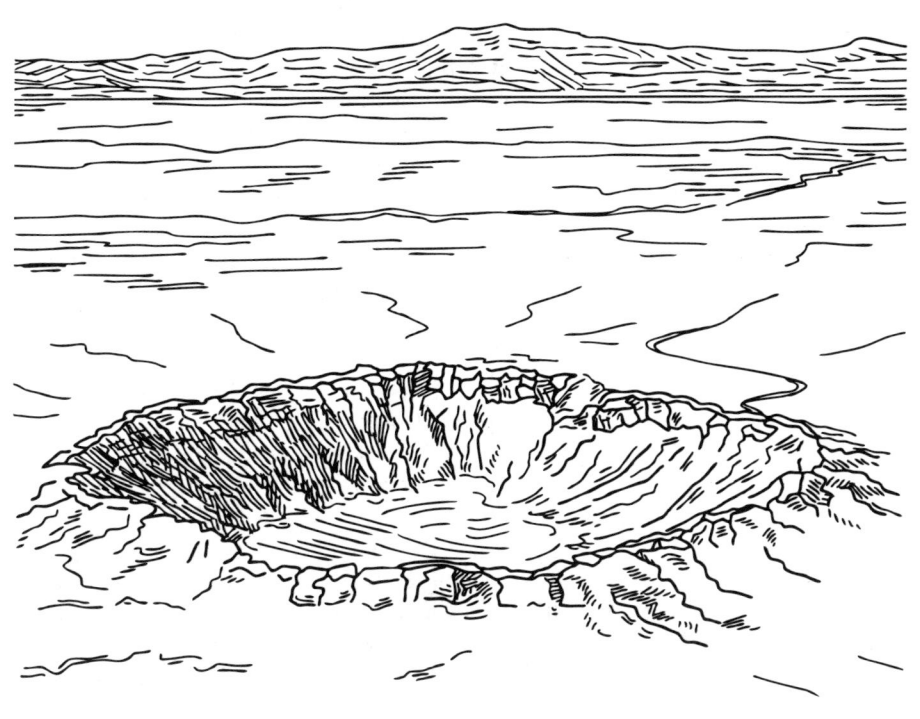

Stream Terraces (D)—Although there is a dearth of permanent rivers within Arizona, several large rivers do exist and these often display stream terraces above their modern banks. These terraces developed within the last few tens or hundreds of thousands of years when the rivers flowed at slightly higher elevations. These rivers left deposits of cobbles, gravel and sand across broad surfaces called terraces. Later dissection by the river lowered its bed and the terraces were left standing above the modern flow of the river. In many instances there may be sets of terraces each descending down to the modern river banks. Terraces are good agricultural settings and many productive farmlands in Arizona are located on these stream terrace surfaces.

*Most stream terraces in Arizona are located in the low elevation valleys of southern and central Arizona. The city of Mesa (**BR**) is actually built on a terrace of the Salt River. Other terraces can be found on the Gila, Bill Williams and Colorado rivers (**BR**). In fact, an interesting set of terraces near Davis Dam (**BR**) record catastrophic floods from the Grand Canyon.*

Earth Fissures (**E**)—Some of the most recent landforms created in Arizona are earth fissures, huge cracks that act as hazards in urban and desert areas. These fissures are the result of extensive groundwater pumping that has drained "fossil" water from the thick stack of gravel and sand that underlies many of the valleys in the Basin and Range. Withdrawal of the water causes the sediment to compact and it collapses downward causing fissures on the deserts surface. Some earth fissures have affected housing developments and farmland in Arizona. These are landforms that may never be seen until they create havoc on the landscape and may be the only ones that are created (or assisted) by man's activities.

*Earth fissures are most common in Maricopa, Pinal and Pima counties (**BR**). Many of them have formed in the southeastern part of the Salt River Valley of Phoenix Basin. A few earth fissures have formed in the geologic past east of Flagstaff (**CP**) and are related to subsidence in solid rock.*

Checklist of Arizona Landforms

Alluvial Fan	18	Impact Crater	26
Arch	12	Lava Flow	24
Ash flow	24	Mesa	6
Bajada	18	Natural Bridge	12
Bolsons	16	Playa	16
Butte	6	Slot Canyon	4
Canyon	4	Spheroidal Weathering	20
Cliff	8	Spire	6
Earth Fissure	30	Stream Terrace	28
Escarpment	8	Volcano	22
Fault	10	Stratovolcano	
Fold	10	Cinder Cone	
Granite Boulders	20	Dome	
Gully	4	Shield volcano	
Hogback	14	Volcanic Neck	22
		Window	12